INSTRUCTIONAL SIMULATION GAMES

The Instructional Design Library

Volume 12

INSTRUCTIONAL SIMULATION GAMES

Sivasailam Thiagarajan
Instructional Alternatives
Bloomington, Indiana
and
Harold D. Stolovitch
Universite de Montreal

Danny G. Langdon
Series Editor

Educational Technology Publications
Englewood Cliffs, New Jersey 07632

Library of Congress Cataloging in Publication Data

Thiagarajan, Sivasailam.
    Instructional simulation games.

    (The Instructional design library; v. no. 12)
    Bibliography: p.
    1. Educational games. 2. Education—Simula-
tion methods. I. Stolovitch, Harold D., joint author.
II. Title. III. Series.
LB1029.S53T47   371.3   77-25458
ISBN 0-87778-116-8

Printed in the United States of America.

Library of Congress Catalog Card Number:
77-25458.

International Standard Book Number:
0-87778-116-8.

First Printing: February, 1978.

Second Printing: August, 1979.

FOREWORD

There probably isn't a single one of us who hasn't played a simulation game and experienced the fun, exaltation, sorrow, and learning that such games have to offer. Sivasailam Thiagarajan and Harold D. Stolovitch will tell you how to replicate the same for learning situations, evaluation needs, and even research efforts.

The thing I most like about Thiagarajan and Stolovitch, besides their humor, is that they always involve the reader in what they are talking about. Here, in this book, you will experience the same involvement. You get to play—and really learn—some simulation games and appreciate the value of others in achieving similar needs you may have for students. You are about to enter into a well thought out, concise description and experience of what this can be and how it can be done. It is obvious that these authors have played the games they write about.

Finally, this may well be the one book in the Instructional Design Library that should really be read in a group setting. Find some other willing souls and try it.

In closing, I would not want to leave the impression that Instructional Simulation Games are intended to produce just fun. Effective learning, approximating the real world, is what the authors seek.

Danny G. Langdon
Series Editor

PREFACE

We have experimented with a number of instructional design formats, and by far our favorite one is instructional simulation games. If we had our way, we would like to teach everything to everyone through this design format. But we do realize the limitations and dangers of this design format, and we have attempted to stress them in this book.

This book contains a number of complete examples, and we would like to thank the numerous content experts and players who worked with us in designing them. The recipes and insights which we present in this book are mainly based on our experiences with players. We would like to express our sincere gratitude to the hundreds of players who provided feedback to improve our games and game design procedures. We are equally grateful to the writings and simulation games of such creative designers as Fred Goodman, Garry Shirts, Richard Duke, Alan Feldt, and Ron Stadsklev.

We would like to single out one particular individual who has been an invisible "guru" to us in this field. For her clear writings, pragmatic presentations, and elegant simulation games, from which we learned so much, we would like to dedicate this book to Dr. Cathy S. Greenblat.

S.T.
H.D.S.

CONTENTS

ABSTRACT

INSTRUCTIONAL SIMULATION GAMES

Instructional simulation games combine a unique set of characteristics which make this design particularly suited to situations where the stress is on interactive learning. This book begins with an actual instructional simulation game and its application to a teaching-learning setting. Once the reader has vicariously experienced the game, an analysis of its critical elements ensues. Various forms of conflict, constraints, closure, and contrivance are examined. A list of ideal characteristics for instructional simulation games is induced.

The book suggests a number of ways in which the instructional simulation game design can be used to attain affective objectives, introduce instructional content, integrate content already taught, evaluate learning, provide a cost-effective tool for testing transfer, and act as a research agent. There is an entire section on the design of instructional simulation games, with a variety of illustrations from such diverse fields as social studies, industrial training, marriage counselling, and meteorology. How to introduce, play, and debrief a game are treated at length. The book contains a number of guidelines for the packaging of instructional simulation games. The authors also describe in detail how this highly motivating design can benefit the *student* by helping him/her acquire complex concepts, new attitudes, and a collaborative working style; the *teacher*, by allowing a higher degree of realism to enter his/her teaching without added costs; and the *administrator*, by providing a vehicle whereby group decisions can be made quickly and with minimum risk. The concluding chapter elaborates a fifteen-step procedure for designing one's own instructional simulation games.

At no time does the book suggest that instructional simulation games are the best design for *all* instructional occasions. Notes of caution and warnings as to when one should abstain from games appear in almost every chapter.

INSTRUCTIONAL SIMULATION
GAMES

I.

OPERATIONAL DESCRIPTION

The best way to describe a simulation game is to participate in one. Rather than wait until you can do this, we would like you to vicariously participate in a simulated simulation game right now. Imagine that you are attending a graduate seminar on interpersonal aspects of instructional development. Members of this seminar have been divided into three small groups of five, and each group sits around a game board with a number of intersecting squiggly lines. Your instructor gives you instruction sheets for the game and explains that each person is to assume different roles. You begin reading your instruction sheets:

HAVE IT Y/OUR WAY

This simulation game is designed to reflect various interpersonal aspects of conflict and collaboration in an instructional-development project. The game emphasizes the clash resulting from each member trying to maximize his/her personal glory while trying to accommodate the needs of the team.
__WHO ARE YOU?__ You are the leader in charge of this instructional development team. Other members of your team include a script writer, a graphic artist, a photographer, and a sound engineer.

WHAT IS YOUR MISSION? You have the job of coordinating the production of an audiovisual training package. This task is simulated by the MIRO board based on a brilliant game invented by Sid Sackson. The board contains a long, continuous dotted line snaking all around, doubling back, and intersecting itself a number of times to enclose areas of different sizes and with different numbers of line segments. The object for your team is to enclose any 25 areas on the board, by taking turns to draw in a specified number of line segments.

Each person in the team has a felt pen of a different color. The person to draw in the last line segment which encloses an area occupies that area by coloring it with his or her felt pen.

HOW DO I WIN? During each round of play, each player accumulates a personal score through individual credits or team credits. All players, including you, try to maximize this personal score. The person with the highest score at the end of the game is the winner.

Scoring in this game is not a simple case of winning and losing. During each round of the game, the team also accumulates a common score. At the end of the 30-minute play period, the total common scores of different teams are compared with each other. The team with the highest common score wins.

There is also an ego-trip score for each team which is the difference between the highest and the lowest personal scores among individual players. The team with the smallest ego-trip score is declared to be the winner on the collaboration criterion.

The team which completes the task of coloring in the 25 areas within the shortest period of time wins the game on the efficiency criterion.

It is possible for different teams to win the game on different criteria.

HOW DO WE PLAY THE GAME? The game consists of three phases. During the first phase you have two strokes (i.e., you can draw two line segments) while all other players have three. Here is the sequence of activities during each round of this phase:

1. Each player has a score sheet which he or she keeps hidden from the others at all times. At the beginning of each round, he or she decides whether to work for personal credits or team credits and writes down his or her decision on the appropriate line of the score sheet.

2. During this phase of the game, the leader decides the entire strategy. He or she tells the other players when and where to play their strokes. All players have to obey his or her instructions.

3. After each player has made his or her strokes, he or she colors in any area enclosed by the strokes. He or she writes down his or her individual credit as the total number of line segments enclosing this area.

4. After all players have made their strokes and written down their individual credits, if any, players compute the team credit. This is simply the total of all individual credits.

5. Each player now computes his/her personal score for the round. Depending upon his or her original choice to work for individual or team credit, the personal score is computed as follows:

	Individual Credit	*Team Credit*
Leader	*Personal score is the same as the individual credit.*	*Personal score is three-fourths of the team credit.*
Other Players		*Personal score is one half of the team credit.*

In computing personal scores from team credit, any fraction is rounded off to the nearest whole number.

6. After two rounds of the game, players proceed to the second phase.

HOW DO WE PLAY THE SECOND PHASE? *The second phase is played the same way as the first one, except for these differences:*

1. The leader still has two strokes, but each of the other players now have four. The leader controls two of the four strokes of each other player. A player may use his or her other two strokes any way he or she wants to.

2. At the beginning of each round, the leader has a team meeting to collaboratively plan for that round. Any player may suggest a suitable strategy, but the leader has the right to reject it and dictate the sequence of play and where he or she wants each player to place two of the strokes.

3. After three rounds in the second phase, the leader flips a coin. If a head turns up, the game moves on to the third phase. If not, the game continues in the second phase.

WHAT HAPPENS DURING THE THIRD PHASE? *The game is played as before, except that the leader can control only one stroke of each other player. He or she still determines the sequence in which different players take their turns.*

Game continues in this fashion until the team encloses 25 areas or runs out of time.

You and the other four members of your team begin playing the game after reading the instructions. You have some problems with the interpretation of the rules in the beginning, but the instructor helps you out. You go in for individual credits in the first round, but decide that your best bet as the leader is to go for team credit. During the second phase, you notice that one player gets very hostile towards you. You point out your altruistic intents and prove your goodwill by arranging the play strokes to provide him with the maximum individual credit during the next two rounds. This makes some of the other players uncomfortable, and they attempt to gang up against him. During the third phase you begin by losing control of all players, but they rally around you later when there are only 15 minutes left and you still have to enclose 15 more areas. One of the players points out that the team score can be maximized by making sure that areas with five line segments around them are chosen and that the person with the largest number of line segments of his color around it be permitted to close it. Another player points out that this strategy also increases the credit for that individual enormously. As a leader you are concerned about keeping the ego-trip score low. You suggest an equitable distribution of opportunities to enclose different areas. All but one player agrees to your suggestion.

You barely enclose the 25th area when time is called. The instructor suggests that each group compare individual score sheets among themselves and determine the person with the highest score. When your team does that, you are shocked to discover that the graphic artist who spoke so altruistically during the game went in for individual credits all the way and accumulated the maximum personal score. Yours is the second highest, and there is a range of nine points between the top score and the bottom one. You are sure that your team is not going to get any collaboration award, but you are impressed by the common score of 53. The strategy for maximizing team credit through completing areas with large numbers of line segments has obviously paid off.

Your team is just beginning to discuss their reactions toward personal scores when the instructor interrupts to compare the scores from different teams. There are three teams and yours is not the most efficient one. But you do win with the highest common score. Contrary to what you feared, your team does not have the highest ego-trip score.

After the discussion of different scores, the instructor announces an open discussion of what was learned from the game. He explains that this phase is called debriefing and it is an essential component of any simulation game. During this debriefing there is a sharing of the frustrations from the game and disillusionment at the end when personal scores were revealed. The instructor asks for players' opinions about how closely the game reflected real-life instructional development projects. The debriefing lasts for about 30 minutes and some players continue talking heatedly even after the class comes to an end.

HAVE IT Y/OUR WAY is an actual simulation game which we designed for use in an instructional-development course. The core idea of having a game within a game to stimulate interactive tensions in instructional development is borrowed from BLOOD MONEY designed by Cathy Greenblat, who in turn borrowed the idea from Fred Goodman's THE HELPING HAND STRIKES AGAIN.

Critical Characteristics of
Simulation Games

Our demonstration simulation game can now be analyzed to identify the characteristics of simulation games in general. Here is a convenient definition of a simulation game to provide us a take-off point for this analysis.

A simulation game is a contrived activity which corresponds to some aspect of reality. The activity involves players who strive to resolve one or more

> *conflict(s) within the constraints of the rules of the game. It comes to a definite closure with the determination of winners and losers.*

There are five C's to every simulation game; each one of them is briefly described below and illustrated with the relevant features of the demonstration simulation game, HAVE IT Y/OUR WAY.

Conflict. All simulation games involve an element of conflict. While there is some argument as to whether conflict is an essential ingredient of all games, we tend to think so, based on various accepted technical definitions of a game. In HAVE IT Y/OUR WAY, the basic conflict manifests itself in each player trying to maximize his or her personal score. There are secondary conflicts which involve getting the task accomplished on time and obtaining a high score for the performance of the team as a whole.

While all simulation games contain an element of conflict, the specific nature and degree of this conflict may vary from one game to another. This conflict may involve competition between players, as in the case of chess. It may also involve competition between teams, as in war games. Another type of conflict requires all players to cooperate against an external threat. Many games which simulate disasters involve this type of conflict. There is also conflict between a player's current performance and his or her previous performance, as in the case of many solitaire simulation games. Finally, conflict could take the form of a battle of wits between players and the game designer. In a simulated fantasy game called DRAGONS AND DUNGEONS, the players attempt to outsmart the person who is running the game in the role of the dungeon master. Obviously, it is possible for the same simulation game to involve more than one form of conflict.

Constraints. A simulation game, just as any other type of game, imposes a number of constraints on the player's behaviors. These are the rules of the game which specify how each player takes his turn, makes his moves, and receives the consequences. As Garry Shirts points out, these constraints are arbitrary and intentionally inefficient. If the object of the demonstration simulation game were for the team of players to color in the required number of areas, the most efficient way is for the players to do so directly. Instead, the rules of the game require them to observe various constraints as to who goes first, how many strokes he or she can make, and who has to obey whom.

The nature of the constraints imposed upon the players may vary from one game to another. There are many minimum-structure simulations in which very few rules are prescribed. The players behave according to their personal choice without violating the rights of other players. At the other extreme, many simulation games in business and international relationships are designed with a multiplicity of rules. It is not uncommon for players to spend many hours and even days reading a voluminous book of rules in order to get ready to play some of these simulation games.

Closure. All simulation games should come to an end sooner or later. At this time, the players obtain feedback on the adequacy of their performances. Generally, nonsimulation games have a fairly simple method of determining who won and who lost, but simulation games make this determination fairly complex. In HAVE IT Y/OUR WAY, the game comes to an end when time runs out or the team completes the required number of areas. This is a very clear closure. However, deciding who won and who lost in the game depends upon a large number of personal criteria. There are many different aspects in which a player may feel that he or she has won or lost in the game.

The type of closure in a simulation game may vary from one game to another. Termination rules for these games may involve a time limit, a target score, or elimination of all but one player. After the game ends, the winner may be determined through different arrangements. Very few simulation games are of the "zero-sum" variety, in which some players can win only at the expense of others. All but extremely simple simulation games have multiple win criteria which reflect such real-life factors as money, fame, personal satisfaction, and chances of future success. It is possible for different players to win on different criteria on these simulation games.

Contrivance. All simulation games are contrived situations. In other words, there are no direct real-life consequences of one's performance in the game. After all, nobody commits suicide if he goes bankrupt in MONOPOLY. While an intense degree of feelings and emotions may be aroused during the play of HAVE IT Y/OUR WAY, players realize it is just a game: No serious person spends his/her time in real-life coloring in squiggly lines.

Correspondence. While a simulation game is a contrived situation, it is designed to correspond to some selected aspects of reality. This critical characteristic distinguishes simulation games from the nonsimulation variety. In HAVE IT Y/OUR WAY, the roles of the players reflect the functions of members of an instructional-development team. The rules for making moves correspond to the pecking order on such a team. The way the game ends and scores are awarded also resembles real-life payoffs.

The correspondence to reality may vary considerably between one simulation game and another. Chess is a very low-fidelity simulation of modern warfare, but it could have been a high-fidelity simulation of ancient wars. Very often, the game may simulate the real-life interactions without simulating the physical reality. The use of the MIRO game to simulate an instructional-development task is a high-level abstraction of the process but not of the products. In some games, the degree of simulation can be so high as to make it almost the "real thing." One of our simulation games, called FORSUM, deals with the evaluation and improvement of instructional materials. Teams of players actually try out short instructional materials on each other and revise them towards increased effectiveness. This situation probably represents something so close to reality that the term *simulation* may be inappropriate. There are other types of high-degree simulation which approach reality from another direction. In a simulated teacher-training game called the CLASSROOM JUNGLE, teacher trainees are given a series of deciphering and computational tasks. Some of the players are provided with the key to the code and short-cut techniques for the completion while others are not. However, none of the players realize these differential resource allocations. The announced object of the simulation game is for each "student" to acquire high scores and teacher approval by completing these assignments. Each player works on his or her assignments independently and announces the result publicly. The game director simulates an authoritarian teacher and pressures player-students to perform rapidly and accurately. As the game progresses, the teacher becomes sarcastic about "slower" students and makes invidious comparisons of their performances and those of the others. After about 15 minutes of this type of intense classroom competition, the teacher stops the simulation game and reveals that some players have privileged information. During the debriefing, the teacher encourages players who were denied the information to share with the others their feelings of frustration and inadequacy. Because of the secret element in this simulation game, players assuming the role of slower children very soon begin to feel like "dummies." From their point of view, this aspect of the game is not a simulation—it is the frightening reality of the inadequacy felt by a handicapped child.

Variable Characteristics of
Simulation Games

We have already discussed how the nature of conflict, constraint, closure, contrivance, and correspondence may vary from one simulation game to another, even though all of these five elements are essential to this instructional design format. Some other characteristics of simulation games vary considerably. Each of these variable characteristics is discussed briefly below:

Replayability. HAVE IT Y/OUR WAY is an example of a simulation game which can be played any number of times without the players losing their interest. Actually, the instructional effectiveness of this game increases with the number of replays. Other simulation games represent single-shot activities because of some secret element in the game. CLASSROOM JUNGLE is an example of this type. Once the players realize that some "students" are supplied with important clues, while the others are not, the game loses its interest and instructional effectiveness. There are many wargames which are repeatedly played hundreds of times by their fans. But, in general, it is very doubtful if any simulation game will acquire the replayability of popular party-type nonsimulation games.

Time requirement. HAVE IT Y/OUR WAY lasts for two hours. There are very few simulation games which last for less than 20 minutes. Some occupy one or two semesters in regular college courses. Within these extremes, simulation games come with different time requirements. Most commercially available games range around the two- to three-hour play period. There are no fast-paced examples which are playable in a matter of minutes.

Equipment and materials. Although computer mediated simulation games are not discussed in this book, there are many people who consider the computer to be an essential ingredient for any serious simulation game. Many complex games in the fields of business and politics do need a computer to provide the consequences for each player move based upon highly complex mathematical models of reality. However, there are many simulation games which use no more elaborate equipment than a gameboard. There are other simulation games which even do not require that.

Number of players. HAVE IT Y/OUR WAY involves small groups of five players interacting with each other. Most of the existing simulation games tend to require larger groups of about 20 to 30 players, which is a convenient size for most classroom groups. There are a few games which require larger groups, and at the other extreme there are some which are playable by an individual in a solitaire fashion. Most examples of the latter type involve a game board and are designed to illustrate the influence of chance factors in some real-life situations.

Purpose. The instructional and motivational purposes of a simulation game are obvious. But a simulation game also can be used effectively to serve a number of other functions. They are extremely useful as testing devices. Results from such a simulation-game test may be interpreted to identify the strengths and weaknesses of the individual, or of the instructional program. Simulation games are also convenient tools for experimentation. They are especially useful for generating and testing various hypotheses about human interaction. More detailed discussions of these uses of simulation games are provided in the next chapter of this book.

By way of summary, Figure 1 provides a list of critical and variable characteristics of simulation games. This list may be

Figure 1

*Critical and Variable Characteristics
of Simulation Games*

CRITICAL CHARACTERISTICS

1. *Conflict*. A simulation game involves some element of conflict.

2. *Constraint*. Rules of the simulation game constrain the behavior of players in prespecified ways.

3. *Closure*. A simulation game has a definite termination and a clear-cut method for determining winners and losers.

4. *Contrivance*. A simulation game is an artificial activity separate from other "real-life" events.

5. *Correspondence*. Elements of the simulation game (e.g., roles, rules, and sequence) correspond to their counterparts in reality.

VARIABLE CHARACTERISTICS

1. *Type of conflict*. Conflict in a simulation game may be between different players, or between all players and limited resources, time limits, or external threats.

2. *Type of constraint*. The rules of a simulation game may be simple or complex.

3. *Type of closure*. A simulation game may end when time is up, or when one player accumulates the target score, or when all but one player are eliminated. Different players may win on the basis of different criteria.

4. *Degree of contrivance and correspondence*. A simulation game may reflect reality at different levels of abstraction.

5. *Replayability*. A simulation game may or may not permit replay by the same players.

6. *Time requirements*. A simulation game may last anywhere from a few minutes to many months.

7. *Equipment and materials*. A simulation game may use complex equipment (e.g., a computer) or simpler ones (e.g., pencil and paper).

8. *Number of players*. From one player to large groups of 20 to 30 may participate in a simulation game.

9. *Purpose*. A simulation game may serve one or more of instructional, motivational, evaluative, and experimental purposes.

---

used as an amplified operational definition of this instructional design format.

Desirable Characteristics of Simulation Games

Before we conclude this chapter, we would like to share our biases about an ideal simulation game. Based on our experiences in designing and using a large number of simulation games, we have come up with a list of desirable characteristics for these instructional activities. This list may be used by the reader in evaluating his or her plans for the first attempt in designing a simulation game.

Conflict. Successful simulation games incorporate a fairly high degree of conflict. However, this conflict need not be in terms of cut-throat competition. Simulation games can effectively reflect the challenge inherent in using limited resources to achieve strategic outcomes.

Constraints. An ideal simulation game has the least number of constraints imposed on the player's behavior. Complicated and lengthy rules are seldom appreciated by players. The designer of a simulation game should attempt to simplify the rules of the game as much as possible and eliminate any superfluous constraints. Complex rules do not contribute to the sophistication of the simulation design. If the rules of a game become too complex, it may be divided into two or more simpler ones. Alternatively, a simplified version of the simulation game may be designed to introduce the basic play; more complex variants may be attempted later.

Type of closure. Effective simulation games end with a bang. Nothing is more anticlimactic than a simulation game that goes downhill and the players then quit. In line with our suggestions about the nature of conflict in a simulation game, it should be possible for all players to win. To be interesting and instructionally effective, a good simulation game has multiple criteria for measuring success.

Contrivance and correspondence to reality. The game should be realistic enough to involve the players. There should be sufficient correspondence between the game and the real-life it simulates so that it is obvious to the most naive player. But at the same time, there should be sufficient safeguards within the game to prevent permanent damage to a player's emotional health. It is dangerous to dabble with intense feelings that are aroused through deception. To a large extent, the success of a simulation game depends upon how easily the players get into and snap out of their roles.

Replayability. An effective simulation game should be replayable many number of times. This permits the players to try out alternative strategies and learn from the resulting differences in the game. Ideally, the game should lend itself to a number of minor variations to keep the players guessing.

Time requirement. A fast-paced simulation game can be very exciting. A slow-moving simulation which drags on forever can be deadly dull. The majority of players prefer simulation games of about 45 minutes duration. This time period fits neatly into conventional classroom schedules and, more importantly, appears to be optimal for maintaining a high level of interest among players.

Equipment and materials. The rate of adoption of a simulation game is inversely related to the quantity, complexity, and rigidity of equipment and materials. While commercial producers may profit in the short term by requiring players to buy specialized equipment or consumable materials, they lose in the long run through consumer rejection. Beginning game designers will have more success with paper and pencil simulation games than with those which require such things as a portable computer or an authentic space suit. There is a current trend to package simulation games as books that have perforated forms and tokens to be torn out. This trend is to be welcomed because it increases teacher acceptance and reduces the price of the materials.

Number of players. Simulation games which involve small groups of three to five players are more flexible than the large (20-30) group versions. A small-group simulation game can be played by parallel groups in a larger classroom, but a large-group game cannot be easily adapted for fewer players. Parallel play by a number of small groups has an additional instructional advantage: The groups can compare their experiences during debriefing.

Purpose. Successful simulation games lend themselves to a variety of purposes. An ideal simulation game should involve aspects of motivation, instruction, evaluation, and experimentation in a proper balance. The designer should keep these different purposes in mind and attempt to accommodate as many of them as possible. An ideal instructional simulation game achieves a perfect balance among the elements of instruction, simulation, and gaming. If any of these elements is emphasized out of proportion, the result is likely to end up as a dull, confusing, and meaningless activity.

II.

USE

Simulation games are so obviously useful for enhancing the motivational aspects of instruction that some of their other uses are frequently ignored. In this chapter we describe and discuss a number of evaluative and research purposes for which simulation games can also be used.

Using Simulation Games for Instruction

Even within the instructional use, simulation games can serve different purposes. Each of these purposes is discussed briefly below with illustrations from HAVE IT Y/OUR WAY and other simulation games.

Simulation Games for
Affective Objectives

Perhaps the most unique characteristic of simulation games is their ability to help students achieve attitudinal objectives more effectively than any other instructional design format. No one who participates in HAVE IT Y/OUR WAY can escape those feelings and emotions which accompany the tension between the need for individual achievement and team spirit in an instructional development project. The same simulation game enables players to experience the frustrations of time pressure which work against deliberate planning. The player in the role of the team leader undergoes additional managerial tensions. He or she has to establish credibility to win the trust of fellow workers. He or she has to face the inevitable hostility toward his or her "easy job." He or she also has to recognize and reinforce individual talent without creating rivalry among fellow workers. While all of these feelings and emotions can be clinically discussed in a printed text, or vividly portrayed in a film, no other instructional design format is capable of permitting participants to actually *experience* them.

There are many excellent simulation games which deal with feelings and emotions in different situations. Garry Shirts' STARPOWER, a simulation game which has become a classic in its own time, powerfully portrays the problems faced by the lowest person on the totem pole in a low-mobility, three-tiered society. Another popular simulation game, GHETTO, reflects the joys and sorrows which exist in ghettos. In this game, players attempt to maximize their "satisfaction points" and realize that such shortcut techniques as hustling have more immediate rewards than longer-range planning and schooling. Players participating in these and other simulation games invariably report a strengthening or a change of their attitudes, beliefs, values, and opinions.

Simulation Games for Introducing
Instructional Content

Simulation games are especially effective in introducing the instructional content for a course. HAVE IT Y/OUR WAY, for example, has been successfully used to introduce a segment of a course on instructional design. The game provides a gestalt for the interpersonal area before each of its elements is discussed in isolation. This game also arouses considerable curiosity among the players about the variables which influence the behavior of individuals in a team. The students become eager to learn the background that would enable them to better understand and control the events which transpire in the game and in its real-life counterpart.

There are many other commercially available simulation games which can be used for this purpose. ORIGINS OF THE SECOND WORLD WAR may be played in a high school class before students begin studying historical facts and figures surrounding that war. Another excellent simulation game, DEVELOPING NATION, provides a preview of the obstacles which affect a country's progress toward the status of a developed nation. This game introduces some of the basic questions to be answered through an in-depth study of Southeast Asia.

Simulation Games for Integrating the Instructional Content

Almost any of the simulation games listed above can be used at the end of a course to provide students with an opportunity to try out the skills and knowledge they have acquired. For example, HAVE IT Y/OUR WAY enables students to plan their strategies on the basis of various principles of team development and interpersonal interaction. DEVELOPING NATION can be used in a similar fashion to tie together individual analyses of the factors influencing the growth of Southeast Asian countries. Obviously, maximum effectiveness may be achieved by playing the same simulation game before and after a course in order to utilize its introductory and integrating strengths.

Using Simulation Games for Evaluation

Games provide excellent performance tests to measure the

ability of a student to transfer and apply his or her skills and
knowledge to a complex situation. The use of games for
individual evaluation of transfer and application is obviously
superior to any paper-and-pencil test and is easier to
administer than a real-life practicum. This principle is utilized
to a large extent in microteaching assignments for the
evaluation of teaching skills and in-basket exercises to check
a person's decision-making ability. Two major areas in which
simulation games can be effectively used as an evaluation tool
are discussed below.

Simulation Games for Transfer Testing

The measurement of a student's ability to transfer skills
and knowledge to novel situations is one of the ultimate
objectives sought in education. Simulation games enable us to
measure a student's ability to do this in a realistic context. Of
course, there are obvious demands on the teacher for
systematic observation and evaluation of student performances and detailed analysis of student score sheets. But the
complexity of administering a simulation-game performance
test is more than offset by its obvious validity.

HAVE IT Y/OUR WAY has been successfully used as a
performance test of interpersonal skills in instructional
development. Results from the test have been analyzed for
various purposes. When the game is played after the course,
a student's scores are reported to him or her as feedback on the
level of his or her competency, with suggestions for improvement. In a practicum situation, these results are used for
selecting suitable team leaders. Another excellent simulation
game for evaluating student performance is DIG. It has been
successfully used with sixth and seventh graders who have
completed a unit on introductory concepts in archeology. In
the game, teams of students secretly create two cultures and
design appropriate artifacts. These artifacts are carefully

buried in boxes filled with sawdust. Teams excavate, restore, analyze, and reconstruct each other's civilization. These activities give the teacher ample opportunity to observe whether each student has mastered the basic interrelationships among such different elements of culture as language, religion, family, government, and recreation.

Simulation Games for Instructional Improvement

Information from student testing with simulation games can be more legitimately and profitably employed by teachers for improving their instructional products and processes. Playing HAVE IT Y/OUR WAY at the beginning of the course serves a needs analysis function for the course. By carefully observing and analyzing the performance of players, we are able to identify those skills which need to be emphasized in the course and others which already exist at a high level. Playing the game at the end of the course enables us to identify the strengths and weaknesses of the instructional experience. Suitable modifications can then be made to the materials and methods of the course to reduce or eliminate major problems and to bring the course closer to its goal of providing a set of practical skills.

Almost any simulation game can be used in this fashion to provide needs analysis and formative evaluation data to improve instruction. Any teacher who has tried to pretest and posttest his or her students has doubtless faced the usual hostility and anxiety. By making a game out of the testing activity, simulations enable us to obtain valid data in an unobtrusive fashion.

Using Simulation Games for Research

Simulations are being used as research tools for studying

complex processes such as anticipated traffic flow in an intersection or the optimum price for oil. They can be used in classrooms for student-conducted research. Neither elaborate mathematical models nor computers are necessary to gain valuable insights through the simplified use of simulation games.

Simulation games enable students to model some aspect of reality. Students may be encouraged to design their own simulation games or to modify an existing simulation game to reflect a different situation. In the process, students conduct surveys and interview people involved in the relevant situation. They develop a summary of these findings in the form of a model and test it against more information from the field. Their understanding of various elements and their interrelationships become clearer.

Simulation games are not limited to survey research alone. In experimental research, these games are useful for generating and testing hypotheses. In a typical play of HAVE IT Y/OUR WAY, each player generates many hypotheses about factors that influence a person's collaborative behavior. Some of the hypotheses from an actual game include the following:

1. The leader in any team is resented by its members.

2. The team leader gains or loses the trust of his crew within the first few moves. If he is perceived as being selfish during the initial stages, a large number of "sacrifices" are needed later to prove his trustworthiness.

3. People are suspicious of those players who talk too much about the common good of the team. These people are usually perceived to be hiding their selfish motives behind altruistic statements.

4. Natural coalitions form between the two or three low scores in any team.

5. Secrecy about one's motives make people distrustful of each other.

6. Time pressure contributes to cooperative efforts within a team. When the pressure is removed, however, members resent their having been exploited earlier.

There is no guarantee that any of these student-generated hypotheses will hold up under continued play of the simulation game, much less transfer to real-life situations. However, these hypotheses form the basis for further review of relevant literature and experimental verification.

Simulation games also permit experimental verification of hypotheses. The findings may not be overly generalizable, but they permit students to pilot-test their experimental design and anticipate results from studies under more controlled conditions. Research with games is conducted by making suitable variations to provide alternative values of a selected variable. By having different groups of players participate in the "control" and "experimental" versions of the game, students may test their hypotheses. To give an example, HAVE IT Y/OUR WAY has been tried out under different conditions of time pressure. In one version, players were required to enclose 100 areas within the 30 minute period—a goal which is impossible on the basis of data from earlier plays. Another version has moderate time pressure (25 areas in 30 minutes), while the third one has no time pressure because the number of areas is not specified. The perform-ances of players are observed during the play of the game through the use of an observation system which records the frequency and the nature of interactions among different players. Players' score sheets are also used as a part of the experimental data. Finally, each player is required to fill out a questionnaire after the game to indicate how he or she felt treated by others during the game. All of these data have been used by the students who ran the experiment to "confirm" their hypotheses that time pressure induces cooperative behavior during the task and resentment after completing the task.

Conclusion

People used to consider simulation games in the classroom as frivolous pursuits used only by lazy teachers who do not take the time to prepare for a more "serious" lesson. This idea is rapidly disappearing in view of the positive experiences of students and teachers who have used this instructional design format. There is some research evidence to support the effectiveness of simulation games, but much more is needed to make an effective case for it. In the meantime, teachers continue using this instructional tool to achieve affective objectives and to introduce and integrate learning into a meaningful whole. Simulation games are also useful tools for evaluating the effects of instruction in general and individual student applications in particular. These games encourage and enable students to undertake experimental and survey research and to gain insights into the interrelationships among different variables.

III.

DESIGN FORMAT

In the first chapter we described and illustrated the critical and variable characteristics of simulation games. In this chapter we will analyze the simulation game into its functional elements. We will then discuss each element in detail and explain the interrelationships among them through several examples.

The basic elements of a simulation game are shown in Figure 2. As you can see from this figure, a simulation game may be conveniently divided into preliminaries, play of the game, termination, and debriefing. Under each of these four major groups we have listed a number of elements. These elements are described and discussed below.

Preliminaries

Students approach an instructional simulation game with a mixture of curiosity and apprehension. Before they begin to play the actual game, they need some background information. The teacher or the game materials should tell them the purpose and nature of the activity. In addition, each player needs to be led into the context of the simulation and assigned a role. The player has to be told about his or her goals in the simulated situation, the resources he or she has, and the constraints under which he or she is to operate.

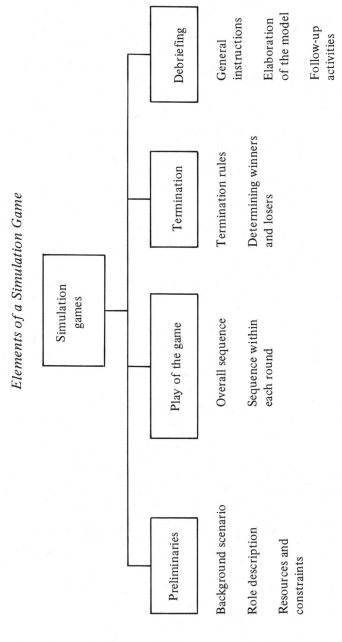

Figure 2

Elements of a Simulation Game

Background scenario. This is a brief description of "the story so far" to provide the players specific clues about the time and the place where the simulated events take place. In HAVE IT Y/OUR WAY, only scanty details are provided because the players are expected to be familiar with the general context. However, in a historical simulation game, it may be necessary to give more details about the period, because such information is of vital consequence in the play of the game. Similarly, a game simulating a different culture needs detailed explanation. However, in writing such background scenarios, the game designer should not get carried away into doing a textbook on the subject. He or she should remember to provide only the necessary information and let the students look up background facts and concepts in other textual resources.

In some simulation games, it may be necessary to provide specific details about background incidents and activities. For example, in a simulation of the legislative process, it may be necessary to describe what bill is to be voted upon and which constituencies are in favor of it and which are against it. Many simulation games begin at a dramatic moment in the midst of a conflict. In these cases, it is especially necessary to trace the development of the conflict. For example, if the game opens on the night before the strike in the factory, players need to know what events and factors led to the strike.

The background scenario may be presented through a printed handout or through simulated newspaper clippings, memos, and letters. The latter approach increases the authenticity of the simulation, but requires a long period of study to organize the information. Another innovative approach is to provide the background through some form of mediated presentation. A brief slide/tape show or a videotape segment can very effectively introduce the context in which the simulation game is to take place.

Role description. In contrast to a nonsimulation game, players in a simulation game are usually assigned different roles. Depending upon the background of the players and the purpose of the game, these roles may be described in varying details. HAVE IT Y/OUR WAY uses just a sentence to describe each role because the player is already familiar with it. However, in some other simulation games, such as GHETTO, there is need for more detailed description of the role. GHETTO provides a background dossier on each person, along with relevant biographical data. This amount of detail is needed not only because the players are unfamiliar with the characteristics of the roles they are assuming, but also because different rules of the game apply to different roles.

One major feature which differentiates a simulation game from a roleplay exercise is the allocation of specific attitudes and beliefs to a player. In a roleplay, the role description may prescribe a specific attitude, as in this example:

You are a young instructional developer with a recent Ph.D. You have been assigned the job of coordinating a media-reproduction team. You are apprehensive and unsure of your ability to assume this leadership role. You do not believe that your profession has any useful answers to many of the problems in instruction. You are also unsure about whether you should be a nondirective change agent or a forceful and aggressive leader. You are particularly worried about the older and more experienced members of your team perceiving you as a college educated "punk" full of irrelevant theory.

While such detailed descriptions of a person's feelings and attitudes facilitate his or her performance in a roleplay, it is doubtful if they should be included in a simulation game. The simulation is supposed to control the factors in such a way that the person feels realistic emotions which naturally arise in the situation being simulated. The power and generalizability of a simulation game depend upon its ability to induce relevant feelings in different people irrespective of individual personalities.

Resources and Constraints

Closely related to the roles of the players is the allocation of various resources. Wealth, power, prestige, competency, connections, experience, energy, possession of raw materials, education, and time are some of the resources associated with different roles. Some of these resources, like prestige and education, are fairly static and may not vary within the game. They may be briefly indicated in the role description. Other resources, like time, money, and energy, have to be invested in various processes during the simulation game. They may be combined and converted into some token form. For example, in GHETTO, the amount of time a player spends on different activities is simulated by distributing poker chips across various activities. In many simulation games, money is a major resource, and this is represented by play money as in MONOPOLY or through transactions recorded in an account book. In a manufacturing game, different raw materials are assigned to players, along with the number of workers.

In HAVE IT Y/OUR WAY, the strokes represent a combination of resources, including prestige, competency, experience, and available time. The fact that the team leader has only two strokes to contribute to the media-production activity reflects the fact that much of his or her time and energy is spent in administrivia, committee work, and drumming up new grants. In some simulation games, play begins with a single type of primary resource which is then used by the players to obtain a number of secondary resources. In the elaborate fantasy simulation, DRAGONS AND DUNGEONS, each player begins with a specific number of gold pieces as his or her primary resource. The player buys a combination of such secondary resources as weapons, armour, magic potions, and flunkeys.

A simulation game should specify the constraints under which each player is to operate. In HAVE IT Y/OUR WAY, for example, staff members of the team expend part of their resources under the direction of the team leader. The sequence in which each person operates is also determined by the leader. Other types of constraints in simulation games involve a limit on the amount of resources spent on a particular activity, modes of communication, restrictions about coalitions, and the factor by which resources are converted into products at the end of each round. These constraints help the designer create various imbalances among different roles to reflect the inequalities of real life.

To summarize, preliminary components in a simulation game include a background scenario and descriptions of different roles. The background scenario provides essential information about the context in which the simulation is to take place and outlines the sequence of events prior to the time the game begins. Role descriptions specify what role a player is to assume in the simulation game without prescribing how he or she should feel. This description may include many of the biographical and personality variables of the character. As a part of the role description, the player is assigned resources to be used in the game, which include such items as time, money, and energy. Also included in the description of player roles are specifications of various constraints under which each player is to operate. These constraints may vary from one player to another depending upon the variations among their real-life counterparts.

An Example of Preliminary Components
for a Simulation Game

Here is a sample set of the preliminary components from a

simulation game called MARRIAGES ARE *NOT* MADE IN HEAVEN. The game simulates how arranged marriages take place among Hindu families.

Players assume one of four roles in this simulation game: father of the girl, mother of the girl, father of the boy, and mother of the boy. Role descriptions for each of these people are incorporated in the background scenario. The reason for combining both of these elements together is to ensure confidentiality of certain pieces of information about prior events.

---

*MARRIAGES ARE **NOT** MADE IN HEAVEN*

You are the father of 22-year old Sekar, who has just got his Bachelor of Engineering degree from a prestigious college. He passed the final examination in first class and you were able to get him a job as an assistant engineer in an international corporation in Bombay using the influence of some of your friends. He has been in the job for three months and his mother is worried about his living alone in a big city 1500 miles away. She thinks it is time to find him a nice girl and get him married and settled down. You also think this is a good idea, especially since you know something which your wife does not. You had a letter from a friend in Bombay in which he reports that people in Sekar's office are whispering about some hanky-panky going on between your son and an Anglo-Indian typist. You know that unless something is done immediately, your family is going to lose the name which it has so justifiably accumulated over the generations.

A marriage broker has finally located a suitable girl who comes from a respectable family of your caste.

> *Both you and your wife agree that she will make a good*
> *match for Sekar, except your wife is a little bit worried*
> *about the girl going to the college. You want the*
> *marriage to take place within the next month since the*
> *times are not auspicious after that for six more months.*
>
> *You are now ready to meet the parents of the girl.*
> *During this meeting you will settle a number of issues*
> *such as the dowry, wedding date, guest list, and the*
> *ceremonies. You will begin this meeting with ten*
> ***compromise chips***. *Everytime you give in to the future*
> *in-laws' demands, you lose a certain number of these*
> *chips, according to the rules explained later. Everytime*
> *you persuade the in-laws, you receive some chips from*
> *them. If you run out of all your chips, you have to agree*
> *to any demand made by the girl's parents.*

Role descriptions of other players in this simulation game differ in the following ways:

1. *Mother of the boy*. She has the same amount of information about her son, except she is not told about the goings-on at his office. She is determined to make the girl drop out of college and to have an orthodox wedding with three brahmin priests. She shares the compromise chips with her husband, but she is not permitted to take any direct part in the discussion between the men. She can listen to the conversation from a respectable distance and may call her husband to the "kitchen" to suggest suitable strategies. She may talk to the girl's mother and attempt to influence her husband indirectly.

2. *Father of the girl*. His girl is a fairly headstrong person with some modern notions. She is 18 years old and is not

interested in getting married for some time. But the relatives are already complaining. The father has three other younger daughters spaced a year apart who have to be married off sooner or later. He is not as well-off as his wife thinks; the expenses of a string of marriages are sure to make him bankrupt. He has 15 compromise chips, indicating that he can afford to be more flexible than the father of the boy.

3. *Mother of the girl.* The mother of the girl has just about the same amount of information, except she knows that there is a flaw in the girl's horoscope. She has bribed the marriage broker to suppress this fact and she is in somewhat of a hurry to get her daughter married before any interfering astrologer figures things out. She is not to participate directly in the conversation between the men, but she may whisper advice to her husband from time to time. She can also speak freely with the other mother.

The one major resource involved in this simulation is the abstract concept of flexibility or willingness to compromise which is the opposite of the prestige which plays an important role in negotiating an arranged marriage. This resource is represented by poker chips called compromise chips. The more chips a family has, the less prestige oriented is its approach. The girl's family has more poker chips to reflect the fact that it has a more flexible position. The boy's family has a lesser amount and they cannot afford to lose face frequently, especially at the beginning of the negotiations. Neither family knows how stubborn the other is going to be because compromise chips are kept hidden. But during the game—as in real life—each family is able to guess how flexible the other is from the way early compromises are made. An overall constraint in this game is the one-month time within which the marriage has to be celebrated. This constraint is simulated in the game by a 30-minute time limit for reconciling all differences of opinion. Other constraints reflect the secondary role of women by the restrictions about how and with whom they can talk.

Play of the Simulation Game

The next set of elements of a simulation game are those which are directly related to its middle part. This includes an overall game sequence, a sequence within each round of the game, the rules which control players' moves during each round, methods of determining the consequences of these moves, and various score-keeping methods and devices.

Overall game sequence. A simulation game may have a single phase of activities, or it may move through different phases. In HAVE IT Y/OUR WAY, there are three phases, reflecting these three stages in the development of a team:

1. The initial stage, during which people perform at less than maximum levels of efficiency. During this phase, the leader provides detailed instructions and the staff members expect specific directions.

2. The second stage, during which staff members become more efficient and the leader relinquishes some of the control. The leader requires and receives more inputs from the others, although he or she still retains the right to make the final decisions.

3. The third phase, during which the leader loses (or lets go of) more of his or her authority. Staff members are more amenable to control through reinforcement and recognition than through authority.

In a historical simulation game, the phases may reflect major events in the time period being simulated. In a game dealing with a labor strike, for example, there are obvious phases related to the events before, during, and after the strike.

Sequence Within Each Round of
the Simulation Game

Each phase of a simulation game is usually divided into a number of rounds. The sequence of play within each round reflects the real-life sequence in a standardized format. Each round of HAVE IT Y/OUR WAY involves players noting down their credit preference, and taking turns according to instructions from the leader. In the simulation game GHETTO there are ten rounds, each reflecting one year. During each round, players first allocate their chips (representing number of hours spent) among different alternatives—work, school, hustling, passing time, collecting welfare, and neighborhood improvements.

To facilitate orderly play during each round, appropriate forms are used in simulation games. These forms serve the additional function of recording the play data for later analysis, debriefing, or research. In HAVE IT Y/OUR WAY and in many other simulation games, players fill out a form to indicate their personal choices, moves, and consequences. To determine these consequences, the game may have various devices from simple formulas to complex tables. The consequences in HAVE IT Y/OUR WAY are relatively easy to determine: Each player gets individual credits according to the number of line segments of his or her color enclosing the area; the team gets the total credit; and the player computes his or her personal score on the basis of the original preference for individual or team credit and his or her status in the team. In other simulation games, computation of scores is more complex. There is often a chance element in some simulation games, which is reflected by a throw of dice or drawing of cards. To combine various individual and chance factors, convenient tables are provided for use by the players.

An Example of the Play
of a Simulation Game

Elements of the play of a simulation game can be illustrated by continuing the discussion of our sample MARRIAGES ARE *NOT* MADE IN HEAVEN.

The overall sequence of the game is a simple one of the two families discussing a number of issues about a marriage. The sequence during each round of the game goes as follows:

1. Players pick a random card from a deck of issue cards. Each card identifies an issue related to the marriage and provides five different positions arranged along a five-point scale, as in the following example:

ISSUE: Dowry
POSITIONS:

1. Since giving and receiving dowry is illegal anyhow, we won't even discuss it.

2. The girl's family contributes sufficient money to set up the household for the newlyweds in Bombay.

3. The bride will bring Rs. 10,000 worth of jewelry.

4. In addition to the jewelry, the bride's family will buy the groom a motor bike and a wrist watch.

5. In addition to the jewelry, the motor bike and the wrist watch, the bride's family will contribute Rs. 50,000 under the table.

There is a total of 25 cards, dealing with such issues as continuation of the girl's education, outfitting the boy's family, guest list, menu for the wedding banquet, number of priests, evening reception, location of the ceremony, order in which the couple receives blessings from the elders, which temple to visit after the ceremony, and rechecking the compatibility of the horoscopes.

2. Each family secretly writes down a number indicating its initial stand on the issue. Wives may offer advice, but the husband's decision is final. After initial positions have been specified, they are revealed to each other. If there is no difference, the players move on to the next issue card.

3. If there is a difference between the position indicated by the two families, they try to persuade each other. The women do not directly participate in this discussion, but they may provide whispered suggestions to their husbands.

4. Either husband may ask for another round of secret voting anytime during the discussion. Players may stick to their original positions or shift to new ones. After both have specified their revised positions, they compare them. The sequence of discussion, revision, and comparison is repeated as often as necessary until players reach consensus.

5. When consensus is achieved, each family compares its initial position with the final one and determines the difference. Each family pays the other the number of compromise chips equal to the number of intervals it has shifted in its position.

6. After reaching consensus on each card, players move on to the next card. The same procedure is used for identifying and reconciling any differences on each issue.

Keeping score during the play of this simulation game is a simple process of trading poker chips at the end of each round. However, to keep the players honest and to obtain a record of the initial and revised positions of each family, the simple response sheet shown in Figure 3 is used.

Figure 3

Response Sheet From
MARRIAGES ARE NOT MADE IN HEAVEN

Issue Card Number	Original Position	Revised Positions								Final Position	Difference
		1	2	3	4	5	6	7	8		

End Game Components

As you may recall from the first chapter, a clear-cut closure with a specific method for determining the winner(s) is one of the critical characteristics of a simulation game.

Termination rules. The rule for ending a simulation game should be based on a logical conclusion of its real-life counterpart. A simulation game depicting the negotiation between a labor union and management logically concludes when they agree upon a contract or when the talks break down and a strike results. A simulation game dealing with the origins of the Second World War ends when the war begins. Many real-life "conclusions" may be translated into game counterparts through one or more of the following devices:

1. *A time period is completed.* A simulation game may have a prespecified time limit to reflect the period allotted for a project. In HAVE IT Y/OUR WAY, the 30-minute time limit reflects such a project period. End of a time period may also be simulated through a specific number of rounds without resorting to a time limit. In GHETTO, players participate in 12 rounds, each of which represents a year. In PLANAFAM, the game ends when all cards in a deck are used up, representing the end of the child-bearing period in a woman's life.

2. *A goal is achieved.* The real-life feeling of accomplishment is reflected in a simulation game through a target score. The game may end when the first player (or team) accumulates this score. Or, it may continue until all other players (or teams) have obtained the target scores. The same idea of achieving a goal is also represented in some simulations through a game board, with spaces for players to move their pieces. This type of game ends when a player reaches the goal space.

3. *A task is completed.* Many simulation games emphasize

neither the time limits nor target score, but require the players (or teams) to complete a task. The task in the game may be the same as the task in real-life (e.g., laying out the front page of a newspaper) or an abstract simulation of it (e.g., completing 25 areas in the MIRO game to reflect the completion of an instructional-development task).

4. *Competition is eliminated.* An unsavory aspect of real-life is the elimination of all competition, as in gang warfare, industrial monopoly, or war. Games which simulate (and hopefully not emulate) these real-life situations come to a conclusion when all but one player goes bankrupt or gets killed.

It must be obvious that different types of closure in simulation games are not mutually exclusive, just as they are not mutually exclusive in real life. It may be possible for a simulation game to have an "either-or" rule for termination. HAVE IT Y/OUR WAY illustrates this: The game ends either after 30 minutes or when a group encloses 25 areas.

Determining Winners and Losers. Many game designers de-emphasize winning and losing in a simulation game on the mistaken assumption of reducing the intensity of undesirable competition. Obviously, if the real-life situation does involve competition, it will be an unjustifiable bias to ignore it in the simulation. Further, whether or not we provide a system for determining the winners and losers, players are bound to compare their scores and comment upon them.

A more effective method to deemphasize undesirable competition is to increase the criteria for determining winners and losers so that they do not become total triumphs or disasters. A serious simulation game will reflect the multifaceted aspects of success and failure in real life by avoiding any simple system of win-lose. HAVE IT Y/OUR WAY illustrates the many different ways of defining success-ful player performance even in a relatively simple simulation:

1. The player with the highest personal score *wins* at the end of the game. This score could have been accumulated either through individual or team effort.

2. All players *lose* if the task is not completed within the 30-minute time limit. This rule emphasizes the need for cooperative action.

3. The team attempts to keep its spread of personal scores as small as possible to *win* on the collaboration criterion. The focus of comparison now shifts to the performances of different teams.

4. The team which completes the task within the shortest period of time *wins* on the efficiency criterion.

Determining the adequacy of one's performance in this simulation game is as complex as in real life. Different players may have different philosophies about the type of winning which is personally meaningful to them. It is possible to encourage cooperation and competition in the same proportion in a game as in the real-life situation with such diverse methods of winning and losing.

Although we have discussed the termination and final scoring in their chronological position in a simulation game, it is necessary to inform the players of these facts at the beginning of a game. Players are apprehensive about how and when the game will end and how their performance will be judged. Providing them with the termination rule and the final scoring system reduces some of their anxiety and permits them to work out their own personal goals for the game. However, this procedure is not without its disadvantages.

When players know that the game is going to end after five rounds or in a few minutes, they increase their scores near the end of the game by behaving in ways which are not representative of real-life behaviors. This type of erratic "end-of-the-world-strategy" by players may undo all the careful design to induce specific types of behavior. In those games where this phenomenon is likely to produce a significant effect, an ingenious solution is to announce more rounds of play in the beginning but to terminate the game earlier. Cathy Greenblat's BLOOD MONEY promises three rounds and concludes at the end of two. While player resentment is likely to occur, they usually see the rationale for this action.

An Example of End Game Components in a Simulation Game

To maintain continuity in our example, let us return to MARRIAGES ARE *NOT* MADE IN HEAVEN and analyze its end-game elements. The termination rule for the game has two alternative criteria: The game ends when all 25 issues have been discussed and decided upon.

A family loses if it runs out of its compromise chips. This is equivalent to the family "losing face" and being reduced to a state of total acquiescence. This result does not necessarily mean a victory for the other family, because such pressure tactics usually backfire after the marriage.

The family which has accumulated more compromise chips (over the number it started out with) wins the game.

The boy's mother scores a personal victory if the families agree to discontinue the girl's education and go for an orthodox wedding. The girl's mother wins if they decide not to double check the compatibility of the horoscopes.

The performances of both families are compared with those of other groups playing the same game. Different teams may score a victory on either of the following criteria:

    a. The group which finishes first wins the game on the efficiency criterion.

    b. The group in which both families have the least variations between their initial and final numbers of compromise chips, wins the game on the mutual give-and-take criterion.

As you can see, this simulation game has a clear-cut termination rule. The win-lose criteria are not so clear-cut but they are based upon a number of relevant factors in the simulated situation.

Debriefing

Although there is not much research evidence to back up the claim, many simulation game designers and users contend that real learning begins only after the end of the game. Debriefing after a simulation game enables the players to think back on their experience, vent their feelings, and relate the game to the reality it represents. A complete simulation game package should include a debriefing guide to help the teacher to effectively conduct this activity. It should contain general instructions to the teacher, an elaboration of the model of reality on which the game is based, and suggestions for follow-up activities.

General instructions. This section should suggest to the teacher that the sequence for debriefing should include a "catharsis" session, logical analyses, and generalizations. The play of a simulation game always generates many hurt feelings, emotions, arguments, and disagreements. Attempting to ignore these and to go directly to an intellectual discussion usually results in hostility among players and toward the teacher. During the initial period for venting players' feelings, they should be permitted to speak out against unfair elements of the game design and the way in which the teacher conducted the game. After clearing up the air, the teacher can move to the more objective parts of debriefing.

Elaboration of the model. As Cathy Greenblat has pointed out a number of times, a simulation game does not simulate reality, but a *model* of reality. A psychologist's model of the same reality will differ from those of a sociologist, a politician, an anthropologist, or a mathematician. Even within psychology, a humanist's perception will differ considerably from that of a behaviorist. It is important that the game designer clearly outline his or her model so that the teacher and the students can compare the simulation elements with this model and judge for themselves if various cause-and-effect relationships hold. Perhaps the most effective method of presenting the model and linking it to the simulation game is through the use of a table such as Table 1. This discussion of the model of reality should include an explanation of what major aspects of "reality" are not represented in the game. The teacher can bring up this fact during the debriefing and prevent any undesirable biases on the part of the learners.

Follow-up activities. The debriefing guide should also contain a list of suggestions for follow-up activities. Here are some sample suggestions from the debriefing guide to MARRIAGES ARE *NOT* MADE IN HEAVEN:

> *1. An excellent film to view after the play of this simulation game is the* **Hindu Family** *(Encyclopaedia Britannica Films, 1952). Although slightly dated, it portrays aspects of marriage customs in rural India. The film depicts the marriage of 14-year-old Donga and has some excellent scenes of the actual wedding ceremony.*
> *2. Another film which may be used for providing background information on the Hindu family is* **The Hindu World** *(Coronet Films, 1963).*
> *3. For a scholarly discussion of rituals and celebra-*

Table 1

Comparison of "Reality" and Simulation in
MARRIAGES ARE NOT MADE IN HEAVEN

Aspect of "reality"	Reflection in the simulation game
Conversations during marriage negotiations are unstructured. Different issues crop up without any logical sequence.	The issue cards are shuffled before the game begins. Players never know which issue is going to confront them next.
Women feel frustrated in this secondary role.	The constraints imposed by women talking only to their husbands or to the other woman and the arbitrary power of the men induce these feelings on the part of the players with wives' roles.
Marriage negotiations involve a lot of give-and-take.	Because there is a limited number of compromise chips available to each family, it does not want not to lose all of them. This provides an automatic limit beyond which neither family can be pushed around.
There are certain issues on which a family may refuse to compromise.	This feeling naturally emerges during the play of the game. To ensure its occurrence at least a few times, one of the mothers is given two dogmatic stands (no college for the girl and an orthodox wedding) and the other is given an embarrassing piece of information to hide (problem with the girl's horoscope).

(Continued on Next Page)

Table 1
(Continued)

Aspect of "reality"	Reflection in the simulation game
Many conflicts are mere questions of semantics.	Players usually define their positions during their attempt at persuading each other. They discover in the process that they both want the same thing but use different words to describe it.
If you keep on winning arguments, you lose in the long run.	During the play of the game resentment against the family, which keeps scoring one victory after the other, is made more probable by the decreasing supply of compromise chips.
During marriage negotiations, it is better for both parties to move toward each other than for one party to change its position drastically.	When there are mutual compromises, both families exchange the same number of chips. Since neither family gains or loses by this move, players feel safer.
Limited number of auspicious days impose a time pressure on the marriage negotiations.	Players have to deal with all 25 issues within a time limit of 30 minutes.
As time pressure increases, families are more likely to make compromises in their demands.	During the game players tend to make more compromises as the clock gets closer to 30 minutes.

*tions of Hinduism, encourage students to read C.G. Diehl's **Instrument and Purpose: Studies on Rites and Rituals in South India (1956).***

*4. For an entertaining account of current changes in marriage customs, have students read the recent novel by India's foremost writer in English, R.K. Narayan. The book is entitled **The Painter of Signs** (Viking, 1976).*

5. Your students may also play Harold Thomas' PLANAFAM I to obtain insights into the related problems of birth control in India. This simulation game portrays the problems faced by a Punjabi couple in trying to achieve an optimal family size.

6. Encourage students to design and play modifications of MARRIAGES ARE NOT MADE IN HEAVEN. You may suggest that the students try changing the number of compromise chips, or the issues on the cards. Other variations of the game may focus on negotiations between the wives or simulate the conflict between a girl with modern notions and her parents.

For an excellent example of a debriefing guide, refer to Cathy Greenblat's manual on BLOOD MONEY. Her presentation of the model on which the game is based is especially effective.

Packaging the Simulation Game

Our description of the simulation game concentrated on the functional elements. The actual packaging of the game involves production and assembly of various game artifacts. Our recommendation is to keep these as simple as possible and to consider the possibility of packaging the entire game in a book format. The most critical element of the package is the player's manual which provides the rules of the game. The following is an example of the rules of a complete simulation game.

RAIN KEEPS FALLING is a simulation game designed to reflect the plights of farmers during insufficient or excessive rains. Weather is the least predictable factor which influences food production and the game simulates this reality.

Number of Players

Literally any number (including one) can play this game. However, the best game is for a group of five.

Time Requirements

About five minutes to set up the game, and from 15 to 45 minutes to play, depending upon the total number of players and the time period they want to simulate.

Materials

Poker chips and a deck of playing cards.

Water-balance charts. There are eight different charts representing different regions in subtropical climates. These charts show the amount of precipitation (rain falling on the ground) and evaporation (moisture returning to the atmosphere) for each month. Differences between these two factors represent the primary amount of water available for use by plants. A sample chart is shown in Figure 4.

Weatherman's calendar. This is a board with 12 spaces labeled with the names of the months. Specific number and type of playing cards are dealt each space to set up the probability and level of rainfall for that month.

Figure 4

*Sample Water-Balance Chart Form
Used in RAIN KEEPS FALLING*

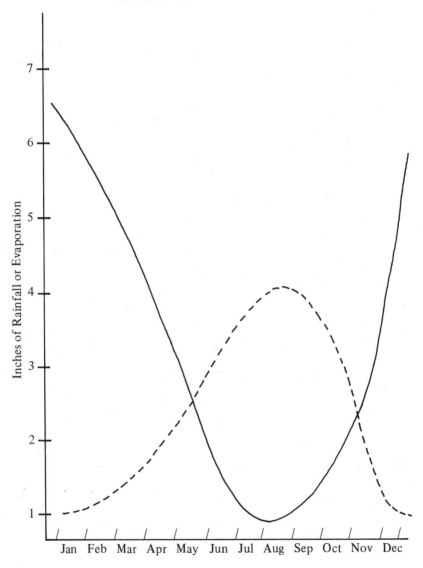

A record-keeping form. This form is used by each player to record his/her allocation of resources and yields from the farm. A sample form is shown in Figure 5.

Brief Description of the Game

The playing cards are dealt into monthly piles, in a partly structured and a partly random fashion to represent the climate of the region. Each player is a farmer with a given amount of resources represented by poker chips. At the beginning of each month, farmers allocate their resources among irrigation, flood control, crop insurance, and raising the crop. A random card is turned over from the pile for each month to indicate the rainfall during that month. The player who obtains the maximum yield for his/her investment over a prespecified number of months wins the game.

Preliminaries

Setting up the weatherman's calendar. Players select one of the eight water-balance charts and distribute the playing cards according to the climatic conditions reflected in the chart thus:

a. Jokers are removed from the deck and the cards are separated into suits and arranged in some convenient order.

b. The solid line in the water-balance chart indicates the amount of rainfall in number of inches. Players list the months in order of decreasing rainfall.

c. Beginning with the month having the heaviest rainfall players deal the number and type of red cards (hearts and diamonds) face up in the appropriate space in the weatherman's calendar according to Table 2.

d. The broken line in the water-balance chart indicates the amount of evaporation in number of inches. Players list the months in order of decreasing evaporation and deal out the number and type of *black* cards (clubs and spades) face up in

Figure 5

Record-Keeping Form Used in
RAIN KEEPS FALLING

Month	Allocation of Resources				Effects of Rainfall	Yield
	Irrigation	Flood Control	Crop Insurance	Raising the Crop		

the appropriate space of the weatherman's calendar according to the same table (Table 2).

e. The red and black cards for each month are rechecked with the table, turned face down, and thoroughly shuffled. The cards are then replaced, still face down, in the appropriate space.

Allocating resources. One player is selected to be the game warden. He or she acts as the weatherman, banker, and supervisor of farm records. At this time he or she allocates 50 poker chips to each farmer.

Making investment decisions and scheduling. Each farmer is told that he/she is growing a cereal crop which requires five months for harvesting. Each player now decides which month he/she wants to plant his/her crop. He/she also has to decide how much resources he/she want to invest for flood control and crop production during different months. He/she writes these figures in pencil in his/her record form. (Once they are written in ink, they become permanent commitments.)

Play of the Game

1. The game warden asks all players to record their resource allocations for the first month in ink. He or she begins with the month of January and checks if any farmer plans to begin his or her planting in that month. If no one does he/she keeps going one month after the other until he/she comes to a month in which one or more farmers want to begin.

2. The game warden collects enough poker chips from all participating farmers according to their recorded investments for that month. He or she draws a random card from the pile for that month and places it face up. He or she announces the weather condition for that month from the following interpretation of the card:

Table 2

Cards for the Weatherman's Calendar

Rank order of the month in the list	Number of different values of cards dealt in the space		
	K, Q, J	10, 9, 8, 7, 6, 5	4, 3, 2, A
1	3	1	0
2	2	2	0
3	1	2	0
4	0	2	1
5	0	2	1
6	0	2	0
7	0	1	1
8	0	0	2
9	0	0	2
10	0	0	1
11	0	0	0
12	0	0	0

	K, Q, J	10, 9, 8, 7, 6, 5	4, 3, 2, A
Red	Heavy rainfall	Medium rainfall	Light rainfall
Black	Excessive dryness	Medium dryness	Slight dryness

3. The game warden checks the food production table and announces the effect of the weather condition on the crops. Each participating farmer notes down this information in his record sheet.

4. The game proceeds in this fashion, with the farmers allocating their resources for each month among irrigation, drainage, and raising the crop. A random card for the month is turned over and the effects of weather are recorded. Whenever the first planting reaches the fifth month, the game warden checks the farmer's records to see if any portion of the crop has been destroyed by weather. He or she adjusts the farmer's original investment in planting by this proportion. He or she then pays *twice* the amount of poker chips as the adjusted investment. (Here is an example of this computation: John originally invests 10 chips in planting. During the fourth month there is excessive rains and he lost 20 percent of his crops. This leaves a balance of eight chips invested. At the end of the fifth month, he receives twice this amount—16 chips.)

5. Whenever the first farmer has harvested his crop, the game warden announces that the effects of weather in future months will be computed not only in terms of what happened during the current month but also on the basis of the weather during the previous months. This is done by adding together the following factors for each of the previous month's weather data:

Rainfall		Dryness	
Heavy	+3	Excessive	-3
Medium	+2	Medium	-2
Light	+1	Slight	-1

6. When the warden returns to a month with a face-up card he or she turns this card face down and shuffles the entire pile before drawing a random card. The game continues as before.

Ending of the game. The game ends for each farmer when he or she has participated for the prespecified number of months. The game warden continues turning up the weather cards until the last player has participated for the required number of months.

Players now count the number of poker chips they have. The player with the highest number of chips wins the game. However, players compare their record sheets to identify other winners on the following criteria:

1. The players who let the weather do the least damage to his/her crop during particularly bad periods of excessive rainfall or dryness.

2. The player who made the best investment in irrigation at the time, thus saving most of the crops.

IV.

OUTCOMES

In a previous chapter we discussed different ways in which a simulation game can be used for instructional, evaluative, and research purposes. In this chapter we shall describe the actual outcomes of using simulation games in educational and training situations. So much has been written about the powerful outcomes of simulation games recently that the reader is tempted to think that this instructional design format is the *ultimate* answer. We do believe in the effectiveness of simulation games, but we do not consider it to be the universal panacea. Great damage is done to the simulation gaming movement by the fanatics who go around proclaiming its unmitigated virtues. Such an approach can only backfire into eventual disillusionment and rejection of this instructional design format. In this chapter we emphasize the negative outcomes of using a badly designed simulation game, in addition to discussing the positive outcomes of planned use of well-designed simulations.

Simulation Games and the Student

Simulation Games Help Students
Learn Complex Concepts
Education today is full of trivial factual learning because

very few instructional design formats help the teacher achieve higher level objectives. Simulation games provide a proven tool to preserve the integrity of a complex situation and enable students to learn skills associated with allocating resources, making decisions, negotiating policies, and resisting persuasion. Experimental evidence indicates that simulation games enable students to make viable decisions under time pressures in a complex environment. The obvious reasons for these outcomes are that simulation games do not reduce dynamic reality to a linear sequence, and that they do provide concrete referents to abstract models of reality. Simulation games filter out the excessive noise of the real world and provide the players with a purposefully structured learning situation.

On the negative side of the same coin, a bad simulation game may simplify complex reality to such an extent that the student gets a dangerous illusion of perfect understanding, while what he or she does not know far outweighs what he or she does know. Such shallow understanding may result in a traumatic shock when the student realizes that the real world does not really reflect the simulation experienced.

Simulation Games Help Students
Attain Affective Objectives

Most of the learning in current classrooms is heavily cognitive. Schools almost totally neglect students' emotional development in their emphasis on intellectual outcomes. Simulation games provide an effective tool for affective growth—the areas of feelings, emotions, attitudes, beliefs, and values. Simulation games help participants gain empathy for real-life decision makers and provide gut-level referents to abstract words. No person who has experienced the frustrations and fears in a simulation game will ever perceive reality in the same way he or she previously did.

There is no doubt that instructional simulation games are capable of producing dramatic changes in attitudes. And this is where a major danger lies. One person's "improvement of attitude" is another person's "brainwashing." Consumers of simulation games need to be assured that the attitudinal objectives of the game are worthy of being attained. Even when a game designer tries hard to keep his or her individual biases from creeping into the design of the game, it is impossible (and boring) to come up with a perfectly neutral game. Many serious users of simulation games are concerned about the issue of biases in games. In a recent article, Cathy Greenblat views with some alarm the potential effects of a simulation game on race relationships which presents a model of high mobility for blacks and a high probability of problems for whites. The student player must later conclude that blacks do not know how to play the real-life game and that this is the major reason for their problems. This is only one example of the fact that a bad simulation game can do great damage through the use of a biased model.

Simulation Games Help Students
Learn Collaboratively

Current classroom activities and grading "on the curve" do not encourage cooperative learning. In contrast, simulation games encourage students to learn together. As a member of a team, the player adapts his individual objectives to group goals. Instructional simulation games help a heterogeneous group of students share differing skills, background experiences, and points of view. These games emphasize mutual learning as an antidote for excessively individualized instruction. In addition, students pick up many social skills related to working in groups and collaborative problem solving.

On the negative side of this coin, many groups have nothing but ignorance and prejudices to share among their

members. Learning in groups is often an inefficient activity
which holds back above-average students. While instructional
simulation games often induce cooperation, a poorly designed game emphasizes a single way of winning at the
expense of others and creates cut-throat competition.

Simulation Games and the Teacher

Simulation games help the teacher to be relevant and
accountable to his or her ultimate responsibility of providing
well-rounded education to the students. Games enable the
teacher to provide a slice of reality to the students without
the heavy cost and risks involved in real-life experiences. The
use of games is more motivating than most other classroom
activities because the student is involved in making active
personal responses. Games enable the teacher to portray
many critical incidents in compressed time. During the game
the class runs by itself and the students learn almost
unconsciously.

From a pessimistic point of view, the use of simulation
games in the classroom offers many new risks to the teacher.
Complaints always emerge from other teachers about the
noise and from parents about "lack of seriousness." It is easy
for the teacher to erroneously equate hectic participation
with meaningful learning. Using simulation games requires an
enormous amount of time and energy. While the payoffs may
be worth these commitments, in terms of student learning,
direct teacher satisfaction seldom occurs. Even the most
nondirective teacher feels neglected in the midst of an
exciting simulation game. Finally, because simulation games
are so highly motivating, the problem of what the teacher
does for an encore becomes very critical. It is easy for a
teacher to turn off his or her students from some conven-

tional modes of instruction because of the success of highly stimulating simulations.

Simulation Games and the Administrator

Many enlightened administrators find innovative applications for instructional simulation games. As an example, one University reports successful use of simulation games for the orientation of incoming students. These new students walk through a number of simulated problem situations in order to familiarize themselves with the administrative resources available at the university. Other administrators report using simulation games to achieve more effective communications in PTA meetings, to select volunteers to work with students, and to involve a larger group in making policy decisions.

Administrators end up having to respond to complaints from committees, teachers, and parents. The high cost and lengthy time investments for simulation games make many people question their cost-effectiveness. Financial committees frequently reject the purchase of any expensive simulation game because such heavy investments in a "frivolous" activity appear unjustifiable. Not all teachers have either the personality or the competency to successfully implement instructional simulation games in the classroom. There is a high frequency of complaints among these teachers against others who use simulation games. These complaints usually attack the excessive noise, the breakdown of student discipline, and the disruption of class schedules. These complaints are reinforced by parental complaints about the lack of serious learning and lowering of standards in the classroom. There is a general feeling that what *was* good, *is* good for one's kids; and, thus, there is an antagonism against new "fads" in education. Parents are also disturbed by the potential effects of simulation games on students' attitudes and beliefs. What the student learns from a game may not coincide with what his or her parents want him or her to believe in. Administrators expect an increase in complaints from conservative communities about teachers' encroachment into the family territory.

Proceed with Caution

We do not want to end this chapter on a gloomy note. While it is true that most of the negative outcomes discussed above are likely to occur, they are far outweighed by the positive ones. Also, intelligent use of carefully designed simulation games will reduce or eliminate at least some of the negative side effects. There are many ways in which simulation game designers can maximize the positive and minimize the negative consequences of using games in classrooms:

1. Game designers can abstain from making tall claims about the efficacy of instructional simulation games. At the same time, they can attempt carefully controlled evaluations of simulation games.

2. Game designers can ensure the integrity of the model used in their simulation games by having it verified by their peers. They can also make the model explicit and discuss its limitations.

3. Game designers can point out the limitations of their games to the teacher and suggest methods of integrating it with other classroom activities through preparing the students and debriefing them.

4. Game designers can keep the cost of simulation games low by providing "do-it-yourself" directions to the teacher. They can facilitate flexible scheduling by keeping down the

time requirement for the game to the necessary minimum and by making each phase self contained.

5. Game designers can abstain from using unnecessary "gimmicks" in the simulation game to impress others. They can carefully eliminate all irrelevant activities—which do not contribute to the attainment of publicly stated goals of the game.

V.

DEVELOPMENTAL GUIDE

In this chapter we present a step-by-step procedure for the design, evaluation, and refinement of an instructional simulation game. At the outset, however, we have to warn the reader that the dynamic nature of simulation game design does not lend itself to a simple linear sequencing! Since it is possible that more than one step in our suggested procedure may occur at the same time, the game designer may have to backtrack in the sequence to refine what was done in a previous step. The 15 steps in the design procedure are presented as a checklist in Figure 6. Each step of the process is briefly described below.

Step 1. Defining the instructional topic. The design of a simulation game must be in response to a felt need in the curriculum rather than an end in itself. Not all instructional areas lend themselves to an instructional simulation game. If one or more of the following student outcomes are desired, there is a strong indication that a simulation game will be cost effective:

a. The student is required to handle interrelationships among a number of variables.

b. The student is required to make rapid and effective decisions about allocating resources and negotiating.

c. The student is required to transfer his or her skills and knowledge to a real-life situation fairly soon.

Figure 6

*Checklist of Steps in the
Simulation Game Design Process*

---

1. Define the instructional topic.

2. Construct a model to reflect the real-life event.

3. Select a suitable game format.

4. Identify the major characters, resources, and constraints.

5. Specify the overall game sequence.

6. Specify the termination rule.

7. Establish criteria for winning.

8. Design a sequence for each round.

9. Write the background scenario and role descriptions.

10. Assemble prototype materials and equipment.

11. Test the game with players and revise.

12. Write the player's manual.

13. Test the game under "hands-off" conditions and revise.

14. Specify the outcomes of the game.

15. Prepare the administrator's manual.

---

    d. The student is required to interact with others in the real-life performance.

    e. The student is required to deal with various strong feelings and emotions associated with the instructional topic.

Step 2. Constructing a model to reflect the real-life event. Once an instructional topic has been identified, it is analyzed into component tasks, concepts, and attitudes. The interactive aspects of this topic are isolated and further analyzed into significant people, and into rules which govern their interaction. All of these elements are synthesized into a model which indicates various patterns of interactions and cause-effect relationships.

Step 3. Selecting a suitable game format. The instructional simulation game designer should be familiar with the wide variety of basic formats for games. As the model of reality emerges in the previous step, the designer will be able to identify a suitable game format or a combination of different elements from basic game formats. This step then evolves into the circular process of refining the model in terms of the game format and modifying the format to better accommodate the needs of the model.

Step 4. Identifying major characters, resources, and constraints. This step returns the game designer to the previous activity of analyzing the interactive components of the instructional topic. The game designer now identifies the key characters in these interactions and specifies the major goals of each. A list of different resources (e.g., time, money, manpower, and raw materials) and another of constraints (e.g., time limits, communication patterns, sequence of activities) is made.

Step 5. Specifying the overall game sequence. Information from the previous step is now operationalized in terms of the overall game sequence. A decision is made at this time about the number of discrete phases the game should contain. The characters and concepts involved in each phase are also specified. Simplicity is an important criterion in creating this overall game structure. If it is impossible to accommodate all instructional objectives within the same simulation game, the designer should not artificially restructure the game. Rather, the additional objectives should be handled in a different game or through various follow-up activities.

Step 6. Specifying the termination rule. It is more effective to begin with the end of a simulation game and work backward than to proceed in the logical progression from the preliminaries through the middle game to the end. Specifying how the game ends provides the designer a criterion for checking the relevancy of all other game activities. The termination rule for the game should clearly specify how and when it ends. This rule should reflect the natural conclusion of the real-life activity which the game simulates. It may take the form of a time limit, target score, specified number of rounds, conclusion of some negotiation process, or a combination of these.

Step 7. Establishing criteria for winning. Closely related to the previous step, and occurring simultaneously with it, is the specification of winning and losing in the game. This step involves translating the players' goals in terms of the scoring system used in the game. The definition of winning may be the same for all players or may differ from one player to the other. Labor and management representatives in a negotiation game may have opposite definitions of a win, while all players in a disaster simulation may have a common definition of win. Another decision to be made about the win criteria involves how many different variables are included in it. As we indicated earlier, an effective and realistic simulation game provides more than one criterion on which the performances of players and teams may be compared. A single criterion for winning a game distorts reality; too many criteria complicate the scoring system and dilute the thrill of victory. An optimum number of criteria can be discovered through player testing. However, a tentative guess has to be made in this step to provide direction for the succeeding steps of game design.

Step 8. Designing a sequence for each round. Based on the overall sequence for the game and the specification of a scoring system, the designer creates a pattern for each round of the game in this step. While some simulation games may not lend themselves to repeated rounds, the majority involve the use of the same set of procedures. Simulation games which contain more than one distinct phase may need more than one such sequence. However, these sequences will be similar to each other, to a large extent.

The general pattern for a round usually contains the following elements:

a. Players make strategy decisions about allocating their resources during the current round. These decisions are recorded and implemented through the exchange of chips and other such activities.

b. Players make their interactive moves according to various rules which prescribe the sequence and relative power for each. This stage may involve structured communications with each other.

c. Chance factors are introduced into the round through such activities as the throw of dice.

d. Consequences of personal moves and chance factors are determined either through appropriate rules or by reference to convenient tables. These consequences are paid off through exchange of chips or adjustments in records.

e. The procedure is repeated as often as necessary until the game terminates.

Obviously, the number of stages from this generalized list and their sequence will differ from one game to another. Further, as we pointed out earlier, some simulation games may not lend themselves to repeated rounds of play.

Step 9. Writing the background scenario and role descriptions. At this stage, the game designer is likely to have a tentative framework for the simulation. He or she is ready to produce a prototype for player testing. A draft of the background scenario for the simulation and description of individual player roles is prepared during this step. The background scenario contains all the necessary information to specify the context and the period in which the simulated events take place. The role description specifies who the player is in terms of such relevant variables as sex, age, educational and socioeconomic background, and other biographical data which are relevant to the play of the game. This description includes the goal of the character, the resources available to him or her, and the constraints under which he or she is to operate. The scenario and role descriptions may utilize authentic-looking documents or a media production (e.g., slide shows or videotape segments).

Step 10. Assembling prototype materials and equipment. This step completes the prototype production. It involves collecting or creating different materials and equipment needed for the play of the simulation game. Game boards, counters, chips, score sheets, dice, timing devices, cards, and payoff tables are some of the different outcomes of this step. All of these items are assembled conveniently for use in the next step.

Step 11. Player testing and revision. The designer is now ready to attempt one of the most exciting and useful steps in the game-design process—actual tryout of the prototype game. Initial debugging of the game may be undertaken with available players, but later stages involve representative players from the student group for which the game is being designed. The prototype package does not yet contain the rules of the game. This is to permit the designer to *ad-lib* his or her way through the rehearsal and make on-the-spot modifications if some problems develop. The designer also participates during the first few tryouts, but does so without dominating the game. Only the minimum rules are provided to the other players in order to prevent any superfluous ones. New rules are presented or created if and when the need arises. During this type of player testing, the designer makes sure that the rules are simple and fair for all players. On the basis of the turn of events, he or she adjusts the relative amount of resources allocated to each player and required for various activities. Payoff tables are adjusted for optimum level of challenge.

This step is actually a composite set of activities which involve testing, refining, and recycling the game until satisfactory play is consistently achieved. The "rule of ten" among game designers prescribes at least ten such tryouts before the game is made available to others. Our own experience suggests that under ideal conditions the designer may end up with an acceptable game in as few as three test sessions, although there is no end to improving a game through player testing.

Step 12. Writing the player's manual. After the simulation game has been debugged and suitably refined through player testing, the designer writes the player's manual during this step. The core of the player's manual is a statement of the rules. The manual may also include background information, instructional objectives and materials, and individual role descriptions.

Step 13. "Hands-off" testing and revision. Many simulation games produce dramatic results in the hands of the designer and fail miserably when others attempt to use it. A serious designer should be able to ensure the playability of his or her game and the replicability of the results when used by others. In this step, the game is tried out by some willing friend or colleague under actual field conditions. Based on reports from the person doing the evaluation, the designer makes finer refinements and simplifies the procedure for administering the game. After a few rounds of repeated testing and refinement, the designer should be able to obtain consistent results.

Step 14. Specifying outcomes. In this step, the designer is able to specify the exact outcomes of the simulation game for its potential users. The list of outcomes is not based on the instructional objectives with which the designer started out, but the actual outcomes during player testing of the game—stated in terms of specific student behaviors. This list should contain any unanticipated effects, irrespective of whether they are positive or negative. Suppressing negative side effects of a simulation game seldom pays in the long run. Game users usually discover these effects sooner or later. Forewarning them to watch out for such effects prevents later disillusionment, and helps players react efficiently.

Step 15. Preparing the administrator's manual. In this step, a comprehensive manual is provided for teachers and other possible administrators of the simulation game. This manual should incorporate the player's manual and provide specific information and instructions on the model behind the game, scheduling the play, setting up the game, conducting play sessions, terminating the game, debriefing players, and conducting follow-up activities. Descriptions of the actual effects of the game from the previous tryouts should be included in a prominent section of this manual.

Many people assume that a simulation game can be easily designed over a weekend. While this may be true of trivial variations of MONOPOLY, the design of a good simulation game requires considerable time and effort. The effects of such a simulation game are well worth the effort spent on designing, testing, and refining it.

VI.

RESOURCES

BOOKS

Abt, C.C. *Serious Games.* New York: The Viking Press, 1970.

Chapman, K., J.E. Davis and A. Meier. *Simulation/Games in Social Studies: What Do We Know?* ERIC Clearinghouse for Social Studies/Social Science Education and Social Sciences Education Consortium, Inc., 855 Broadway, Boulder, Colorado, 80302, 1974.

Duke, R.D. *Gaming: The Future's Language.* New York: John Wiley & Sons, Halsted Press Division, 1974.

Gordon, A.K. *Games for Growth: Educational Games in the Classroom.* Chicago: Science Research Associates, 1972.

Greenblat, C.S. and R.D. Duke. *Gaming-Simulation: Rationale, Design, and Applications.* New York: Halsted Press, 1975.

Heyman, M. *Simulation Games for the Classroom.* Bloomington, Indiana: Phi Delta Kappa, 1975.

Livingston, S.A. and C.S. Stoll. *Simulation Games: An Introduction for the Social Studies Teacher.* New York: Free Press, 1973.

Maidment, R. and R.H. Bronstein. *Simulation Games: Design and Implementation.* Columbus, Ohio: Charles E. Merrill Publishing Co., 1973.

Stadsklev, R. *Handbook of Simulation Gaming in Social Education, Part One, Textbook.* Institute of Higher

Education Research and Service, The University of Alabama, Box 6293, University, Alabama, 35486, 1974.

Taylor, J.K. and R. Walford. *Simulation in the Classroom.* Baltimore: Penguin Books, 1972.

Twelker, P.A. and K. Layden. *Educational Simulation/ Gaming.* Stanford, California: ERIC Clearinghouse on Media and Technology, 1972.

JOURNALS

Simulation and Games: An International Journal of Theory, Design, and Research. Published by Sage Publications, 275 South Beverly Drive, Beverly Hills, California 90212.

Simulation/Gaming. Published by Simulation/Gaming News, Box 3039, University Station, Moscow, Idaho 83843.

DIRECTORIES

Belch, J. *Contemporary Games, Volume I (Directory).* Detroit: Gale Research, 1973.

Stadsklev, R. *Handbook of Simulation Gaming in Social Education, Part Two, Directory.* Institute of Higher Education Research and Service, The University of Alabama, Box 6293, University, Alabama 35486, 1975.

Zuckerman, D. and R.E. Horn. *The Guide to Simulations/ Games for Education and Training.* Lexington, Mass.: Information Resources, Inc., 1973.

SIVASAILAM ("Thiagi") THIAGARAJAN began his career in education in Madras, India, where he taught high school physics and math for six years. His home-grown instructional innovations attracted the attention of Dr. Douglas Ellson, who invited him to come to the United States and work for him. Thiagarajan received his Ph.D. in Instructional Systems Technology from Indiana University. His professional experiences in the United States include administering six major instructional developmental projects, consulting with 40 organizations, serving on the editorial board of six professional journals, participating in national and international advisory panels, and conducting more than 60 workshops all over the country. Thiagarajan has published six books and more than 40 articles on different aspects of instructional and performance technology, and has produced 30 audiovisual training modules and 15 simulations/games.

HAROLD D. STOLOVITCH has taught children and adults in a number of different settings and cultures for more than 15 years. A fluent speaker of English and French, he has conducted extremely successful courses and workshops in various parts of Africa, the United States, and Canada. He is the designer of a number of games and author of articles on simulations/games as well as various aspects of instructional development and evaluation. He is currently at the Universite de Montreal, where he teaches courses and directs research on instructional technology. Earlier, at Indiana University, he taught a graduate course on the design, evaluation, and use of simulations/games.